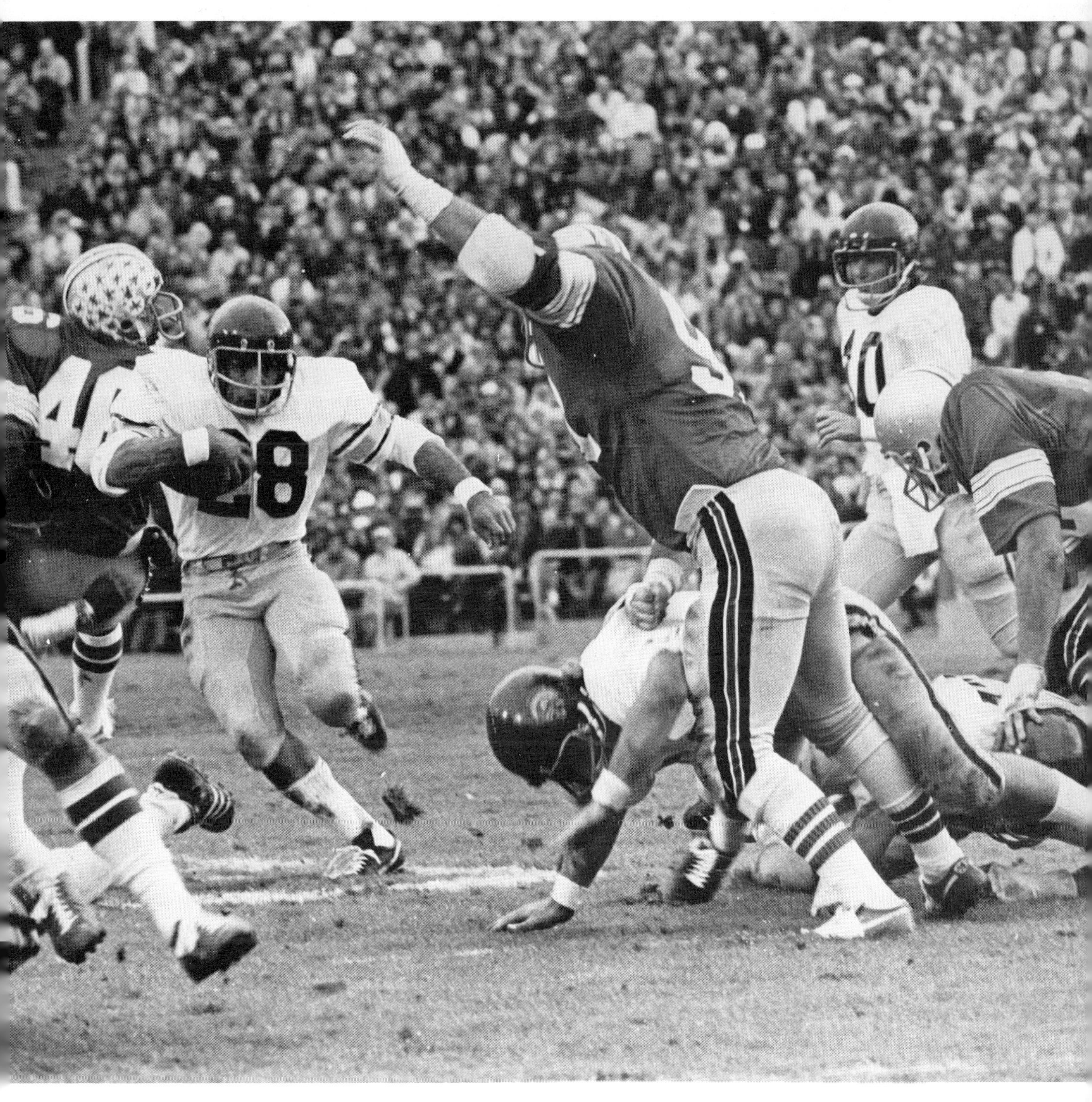

The colorful Rose Parade takes place before the annual Rose Bowl football game. Flower-covered floats have been a tradition since the 1890's.

SPORTS CLASSIC

THE ROSE BOWL

By JULIAN MAY

Creative Education
Childrens Press

Photograph and Illustration Credits

PHOTO CREDITS:

UPI 22, 30, 33, 34, 37, 39, 40, 44, 45
Tournament of Roses 1, 2, 8, 11, 17, 19, 46
Acme Photo 12, 15, 21, 25, 27
McCausland Photo .... Cover, 43

Published by Creative Educational Society, Inc., 123 South Broad Street, Mankato, Minnesota 56001. Printed in the United States.

Library of Congress Cataloging in Publication Data

May, Julian.
The Rose Bowl.
SUMMARY: A brief history of the Tournament of Roses and the Rose Bowl game with details of games of recent years.
1. Rose Bowl Game, Pasadena, Calif. — Juvenile literature.
[1. Rose Bowl Game, Pasadena, Calif. 2. Football] I. Title.
GV957.R6M38 796.33'272 76-8459 ISBN 0-87191-521-9

Contents

Tournament of Roses

It is a gigantic New Year's greeting to the whole country from a California city.

Every January First, the streets of Pasadena fill with marching bands, splendid horseback riders, smiling celebrities, and fantastic floats decorated with living flowers. Crowds gape at the spectacle from the sidelines. Millions more, all over the United States, admire the pageant on television.

After the parade, there is a college football game, an annual classic that is the granddaddy of all Bowl games. The Tournament of Roses tries to pit the best West Coast team against the best Big 10 college team from the East. Every New Year's Day, the Rose Bowl Stadium is packed with cheering fans. Some of them had purchased their tickets as much as 10 years ago so that they would be sure of a place in the Pasadena sun.

In the beginning, however, there were only the roses. A zoologist named Charles Frederick Holder came to live in sunny Pasadena back in the late 1800's. It was just a small town then, with dirt streets; but flowers bloomed all through the winter when much of the rest of the United States was buried in snow.

Professor Holder loved Pasadena and wanted to tell the world about its beauty. He urged civic leaders to have a flower festival, and they agreed. The first Tournament of Roses was held on January 1, 1890. Local citizens decorated their horse-drawn carriages with flowers and paraded proudly along

Hopeful Stanford boys pose with local beauties before the first Rose Bowl game in 1902.

Roses of victory went to this Michigan team in 1902. The coach (top row, center) is Fielding H. "Hurry Up" Yost.

the main street. After the parade, there were foot races, pony races, "orange races," and other amateur sports. People ate picnic lunches under the huge oak trees. The Tournament of Roses was such a success that it was decided to make it an annual event.

The festival grew bigger every year. Gaily-dressed horseback riders and automobiles covered with flowers joined the decorated carriages. Floats began to appear in 1894. Marching bands and out-of-town entries joined the parade. Tourists filled Pasadena hotels; but they came to see the Rose Parade, not the simple sporting events that followed.

"We need a sports attraction that will get people in the icy East and North talking!" declared the Tournament president, James B. Wagner. "We need a football game!"

The hottest team in the East in 1901 was Michigan's Wolverines. They had won 10 straight games and were called the "point-a-minute wonders." The West Coast's best team, California's Berkeley Bears, declined the Pasadena invitation; so the Tournament turned to Stanford.

Tournament Park had 1,000 seats, but they were far from sufficient. A mob of over 8,000 fans swarmed over the fences and onto the playing field to watch that first game in Rose Bowl history, played January 1, 1902.

They saw Michigan score 8 touchdowns (5 points each), 1 field goal (5 points), and 4 conversions (1 point each) for a total of 49 points. Stanford scored nothing.

The local newspaper tried to put a good face on things. One writer burbled, "Never was there a fairer day in this land of sunshine and flowers!"

But he was talking about the weather, not the football game. The local people were so disappointed at the clobbering of their western team that Tournament officials decided to forget about football.

For the next 13 years, the Tournament of Roses featured other sporting events. There were polo games, chariot races — even ostrich races! A larger stadium was built, but the oddball sports failed to attract a large audience. People came to see the parade but stayed away from the games.

"Chariot races are all very well," one man said, "but this isn't ancient Rome. It's America. And America's favorite sport is football!"

So in 1916, the Tournament of Roses revived its East-West pigskin battle. Big-time eastern colleges declined to travel the long distance to Pasadena. The Tournament had to make do with Brown University. The honor of the West was represented by Washington State. Washington won, 14-0.

Unseasonable rain and Brown's second-rate status held the crowd to only 7,000. The game lost money; and even worse, it attracted no national attention.

But the following year, the Tournament was able to book two truly top teams — the University of Pennsylvania and Oregon. This time, 25,000 fans packed the stadium to cheer as Oregon upset the powerful Easterners, 14-0. The game made headlines all over the country, and football had come to stay in the Tournament of Roses.

Chariot races were featured at the Tournament of Roses from 1903 until 1915.

Some 30,000 cars jammed parking lots around the Rose Bowl during the late 1930's.

During World War I, the game was fought by teams from the armed services. A young sailor who played for the winning Great Lakes Naval Training School team in 1919 never forgot his victory.

"Playing in the Rose Bowl was one of the greatest thrills of my life," George Halas said later. But the man who later became coach and owner of the NFL Chicago Bears had a faulty memory. It wasn't called the Rose Bowl yet!

Until 1923, all the games were played in Tournament Park. The game became so popular, however, that the officials knew they would have to build a new stadium. It was to be patterned after the famous Yale Bowl of the East. A Pasadena reporter named Dusty Hall dreamed up a name for the new football shrine. He called it the Rose Bowl.

Today the enlarged and expanded Rose Bowl Stadium accommodates more than 100,000 spectators at the annual football classic, and college fans are in suspense every fall as they await the voting that will decide which teams will play. The Rose Bowl game has become a college football institution — the oldest and best Bowl game of them all!

Four Horsemen of the Rose Bowl

They came galloping out of the East – out of South Bend, Indiana, and Notre Dame University, that is. They were a football legend, Coach Knute Rockne's great backfield known as the Four Horsemen.

The Fighting Irish of 1924 had one of the greatest college teams in history. They were undefeated, largely due to the talents of the magnificent Four – quarter-back Harry Stuhldreher, fullback Elmer Layden, right halfback Don Miller, and left halfback Jim Crowley.

On New Year's Day, 1925, the Four Horsemen played their last college game. Their opponent was Stanford, also undefeated, but tied once that season. Stanford's star was Ernie Nevers, a blond, massive fullback, famous for trampling rival defensemen. Its coach was the immortal Glenn "Pop" Warner. The contest promised to be an epic one, and 53,000 fans crowded the Rose Bowl to be in on the excitement.

As the game opened, Coach Rockne sent in his secondary team, the "shock troops," to test Stanford's offense. (This was before the days of two-platoon football.) The explorers proved that Stanford's Indians were very tough indeed.

When the second squad retired, out came Notre Dame's first team – the vaunted Four Horsemen and their Seven Mules. Stanford was alert when Miller fumbled the ball. The Indians' Charley Johnson recovered on the Notre Dame 17. Then the

Each year's parade features a Rose Queen.
Ruling in 1937 was Nancy Bumpus (center).

tanklike Nevers took over, setting up a field-goal try for Stanford. The boot was good, and the West Coast team led, 3-0.

The Four Horsemen began a delayed gallop. Layden went in for a touchdown, and it was 6-3, Notre Dame. The fleet, skinny Layden scored again before the half ended, intercepting a Nevers pass and running it 78 yards to the end zone. Coming into the third period, it was Notre Dame 13, Stanford 3.

But the Indians never let up, sending the mighty Nevers rushing against the Irish for good yardage. Twice Stanford set up field goals and failed. Then Layden booted a spiral 50 yards upfield, where a Stanford safety lost it in the sun. Irish end Ed Hunsinger nailed it and ran 20 yards for a TD. A good kick made the score 20-3.

Like a wild man, Nevers strove to bring his team from behind. He would carry the ball 34 times for 114 yards in the game even though both his ankles were injured. He intercepted a Stuhldreher pass and battered his way in play after play to the Irish 1-yard line.

Notre Dame built a stone wall, but the surprising Stanford team passed for a touchdown! With the kick, it was 20-10.

In the fourth quarter, Stanford fought to the Irish goal-line again. Nevers made a dive toward the end zone as the fans howled joyfully. But according to the ref, he fell inches short of a touchdown! The crowd screeched in disbelief, and arguments would rage for years about that call.

In the last 25 seconds of the game, Layden ran another interception 70 yards for a final TD, making it 27-10. But California fans knew it might have turned out differently if Nevers' "touchdown" had been allowed.

Jim Crowley carries the ball for Notre Dame during the 1925 Rose Bowl game.

The Greatest Football Blunder

What was the worst mistake ever made in a college football game? A lot of people think it happened in the Rose Bowl in 1929 when Georgia Tech played California in a game that had the whole country talking.

Georgia Tech was undeafeated that season, while the California team had lost one and tied one. The captain-elect of the Golden Bears was center Roy Riegels, a fine player who would attain gridiron immortality in a very strange way.

The enlarged Rose Bowl was packed with 71,000 fans, and the game was broadcast coast-to-coast on radio. At the beginning of the second quarter the teams changed sides. There was still no score. Stumpy Thomason of Georgia Tech had the ball but fumbled when he was hit by the Bears' Benny Lom.

Under the rules of the day, the ball was free. Roy Riegels swooped in, grabbed it, and took off. He began a 65-yard run toward the goal-line as the fans rose up and began to yell. Benny Lom ran behind him, shouting. Other California players joined in, only to be dragged down by Georgia men who were carefully protecting the charging Riegels BECAUSE ROY RIEGELS WAS RUNNING THE WRONG WAY.

With Lom still pursuing, Roy went into the end zone. Benny turned him around, and he was finally stopped on the 1-yard line. Lom's punt bobbled and became a 2-point safety, and Georgia went on to win, 8-7.

Later, a rule change prohibited advancing a fumble that hits the ground; but the change came too late for Roy Riegels, "Mister Wrong Way" of the Rose Bowl.

Roy Riegels, shepherded by Georgia Tech players, makes his unforgettable run in 1929.

The Perfect Play

In 1939, the Stanford Indians won only a single game. So the team got a new coach, Clark Shaughnessy. He came from the University of Chicago with a perfect season record, all losses.

But to the surprise of one and all, Coach Shaughnessy turned the Stanford losers completely around. His secret — the T-formation with a man in motion. Today, when this play is almost universal, it is hard to realize that it was a brand-new idea in 1940. The Chicago Bears of the NFL had been using the T, and Shaughnessy had learned it from George Halas while serving as a part-time coach for the Monsters of the Midway.

Out at Stanford, Shaughnessy taught his quarterback, Frankie Albert, how to mislead the opposition by handing off to other backs rather than bulling through with the ball himself. The coach taught the brushblock and the end-around run. These were revolutionary in 1940.

The lowly Indians went out, armed with their new techniques, and won nine games in a row. Then they took their T-formation to the Rose Bowl and played one of the most influential of all college games.

Stanford's opponent was Nebraska. The Cornhuskers had been beaten only once, and they were considered very tough. Four minutes after taking possession of the ball, Nebraska got on the scoreboard with a touchdown.

Stanford's great coach, Clark Shaughnessy, caused a revolution in college football.

Vike Francis of Nebraska (38) scores early in the 1941 Rose Bowl game. Stanford's Pete Kmetovic (17) and Stan Graff (41) stand by helplessly.

Right halfback Hugh Gallarneau gallops for a Stanford touchdown, shepherded by quarterback Frankie Albert (19).

"Don't worry, Coach!" yelled Frankie Albert. "We haven't had the ball yet!"

The T-formation was revealed in all its glory as the Indians took the offensive. Left halfback Pete Kmetovic went 29 yards to the Nebraska 18, then on to the 9. Then the right halfback, Hugh Gallarneau, went over for a touchdown.

In the second period, Nebraska scored again, making it 13-7. The Indians came back with a 40-yard pass play and led at the half, 14-13.

The second half was destined to belong to Stanford. The Indians marched to the Nebraska 1-yard line, where the Cornhuskers made a valiant stand and took the ball on downs. From deep in the end zone, Husker Harry "Hippity" Hopp punted. Kmetovic of Stanford caught the ball on the Nebraska 39.

Defenders closed in on him, but he darted left, then right, and confused the Nebraska players. Each Stanford man now performed the blocking chore that Coach Shaughnessy had worked so hard to teach.

Whammo! All eleven of the Nebraska players bit the dust! (Albert got two). Kmetovic raced toward the goal and scored on a perfect play. The final score was 21-13, Stanford.

The expert use of the T-formation astounded football fans and coaches alike. After that memorable New Year's Day, college teams all over the country abandoned their old-fashioned formations and went with the T.

It was a genuine football revolution, and it all started at the Rose Bowl.

PAC-8 Versus Big 10

Who plays in the Rose Bowl?

The original Tournament criterion was informal: "The best team in the West will play the best team in the East." But it didn't always work out that way. Top teams often declined Bowl bids for one reason or another, and many of the early games were played by also-rans.

There was also a feeling among some eastern colleges that post-season Bowl games were "commercial events" and therefore just a bit tainted. The lofty pronouncement was made, "We play football for fun, not for money. We don't want an overemphasis on the game."

During the years of turmoil, Big 10 schools removed themselves from Rose Bowl contention even though their teams were often ranked No. 1 in the nation. But alumni and fans kept pressing for a change in policy. From 1921 until 1947, no Big 10 teams played in the Pasadena classic.

After World War II ended, peace came to the gridiron war as well. The 26-year deadlock was broken, and it was agreed that henceforth, Rose Bowl participants would be chosen from the Pacific Coast Conference and from the Big 10. No Big 10 team could play two years in a row (a rule that was later rescinded). The teams would share in the profits equitably.

Beginning with the 1947 contest of UCLA vs. Illinois, it would be Pac-8 against Big 10 all the way.

In 1945, USC beat Tennessee 25-0. Here Tennessee fullback Mark Major is stopped by the Trojan line.

Rose Bowl Upset

The Rose Bowl Committee had looked upon their "marriage" of the Big 10 and the Pac-8 as a great triumph. As years passed, however, they must have had mixed feelings; for Big 10 teams dominated the Rose Bowl for nearly 20 years. Between 1947 and 1966, eastern teams won 15 games and western teams only 4.

Pacific Coast humiliation reached a low point in 1965. Michigan not only mashed Oregon State 34-7, but also sent its mascot, a pig named Cleopatra, out to make a scoring run! The pig was tackled by a fan. A newspaper noted wryly, "If the fan came from Oregon State, he made the best Oregon tackle of the day."

The Oregon coach, Tommy Prothro, moved on to UCLA the next season. There he would coach the team that avenged all the western defeats in a classic game that would signal the start of a new Rose Bowl era.

The 1966 Big 10 Rose Bowl bid went to powerful Michigan State, undefeated that season. The western contender was Prothro's UCLA, 7-2-1 that year. No one gave the scrappy UCLA Bruins a chance against the Michigan Spartans. The Bruins looked like midgets as they lined up against the massive Spartan squad.

The Michigan team (striped helmets) punches toward USC's one-yard line on the way to a 1948 Rose Bowl victory of 49-0.

Courage and discipline seemed to be all that UCLA had going for it. The Bruins held Michigan State scoreless in the first quarter. In the second, the Spartans fumbled a punt on their own 6-yard line. A Bruin fell on the ball, and UCLA took over.

Bruin quarterback Gary Beban, a sophomore star, then shocked the fans by executing a sneak! He

went scrambling into the end zone for a touchdown. The Bruins converted, making it 7-0.

Next UCLA's Kurt Zimmerman executed an on-side kick-off, which was recovered on the Michigan State 42. Five plays later, Beban fired a bomb pass to end Kurt Altenburg on the Spartan 1. Bubba Smith and the rest of the huge Michigan line closed in, but Beban once again took the ball himself and dove over to score.

Zimmerman's kick was good; and it was 14-0, UCLA.

The second half saw the valiant Bruin defense take the ball away from Michigan three times on fourth downs. UCLA also recovered two fumbles and intercepted three passes. The most heroic Bruin defender was little Bob Stiles, only 5-feet-9 and 170 pounds. His greatest moment came in the last 31 seconds of the game.

Michigan had just scored its second TD. The Spartans elected to try for a 2-point ground conversion that would tie the game. Reserve quarterback Jim Raye, a pitch-out whiz, came in and sent the ball to 212-pound Bob Apisa, who darted around right end.

Apisa bulled toward the goal line, shedding the little Bruin defensemen like drops of water. Then Bob Stiles attacked! He leaped onto Apisa's back, and the big Spartan went down inches from the goal, crushing Bob Stiles beneath him.

UCLA won, 14-12; and the fans cheered themselves hoarse for Stiles, who would be named Player of the Game. But gallant Bob didn't hear a thing. He had been knocked cold as he made the Big Save.

A Buckeye Blast

The Tournament of Roses had a big temptation the next season. The NFL and the AFL had decided to stage the first Super Bowl in 1967; and they wanted to do it in Pasadena's Rose Bowl stadium, a week after the classic college game!

It would mean a lot of money for the town. But everyone knew that the pro title tilt would take the spotlight away from the college Rose Bowl game, and college football had made Pasadena famous. The town and the Tournament decided to remain loyal to the kind of football they knew best. It was decreed that no Super Bowl game would ever be played in Pasadena.

The year 1967 also marked the first of four straight Rose Bowl appearances by the University of Southern California. USC, coached by the great John McKay, had a heart-breaking 14-13 loss to Purdue that year. But the next season was something else!

The Trojans acquired a great new runner, a fellow named O. J. Simpson. O. J. had long dreamed of playing in the Rose Bowl, but poor grades had forced him to attend a Junior College for two years. Then he transferred to USC. In the 1968 Rose Bowl, O. J. Simpson scored both touchdowns as USC beat Indiana, 14-3.

The next season, USC and O. J. were back. This time, their opponent was Ohio State, rated No. 1 in the nation. USC was rated No. 2, and it was the first time that the two best college teams had played in the Rose Bowl. Over 100,000 fans crowded in to see the game.

O. J. Simpson with the Heisman Trophy, awarded to him as top college football player of 1968.

It started off great for the Trojans. In the first quarter, USC scored with a 21-yard field goal and an 80-yard dash by Simpson. It was 10-0, USC.

Buckeye quarterback Rex Kern tongue-lashed his Ohio teammates in the huddle. "Why don't we quit messing around and get to work?" he snapped.

Kern, just recovered from an injury, was not yet able to play his best; but what he had was good enough. He marshalled a drive that bought 69 yards in 13 plays with a TD at the end of the line. It was 10-7 with less than 2 minutes in the half.

The Trojans kicked off; but their quarterback got sacked, and they took time out. When they had to punt, the Buckeyes had a minute to play with. They used it on a surprise set of pass plays that got a first down on the USC 16! Pressing closer and closer, they were still short with only 3 seconds remaining; so the Buckeyes went for a field goal, sank it, and tied the score, 10-10, at the half.

The third quarter saw Trojan quarterback Steve Sogge lose the ball on a fumble, putting Ohio on USC's 21-yard line. Two plays later the Bucks had a touchdown. Then it was O. J.'s turn to get squeezed. He fumbled behind the line of scrimmage and set up still another Buckeye touchdown, making it 24-10.

The romping Buckeyes kicked another field goal. Then came a last Trojan touchdown on a disputed call deep in the end zone for a final score of 27-16.

Woody Hayes's Buckeyes were voted Team of the Decade. USC slunk away, still No. 2, and resolved to try harder.

Mission Impossible

In 1970, both USC and Ohio State were headed for the Rose Bowl again. The Trojans made it, but the luckless Bucks were sunk on the last day of the season when an underdog Michigan team beat them, 24-12.

So Michigan went to the Rose Bowl, where it was greeted with a short poem:

Oh, goodie!
No Woody!

P.S.: USC beat Michigan 10-3.

In 1971, Ohio State was back, heavily favored to win. One pre-game banquet featured the star of TV's "Mission Impossible" program, who said, "I assure you this Ohio State team will not self-destruct!" Stanford, the year's West Coast champ, was a decided underdog.

The biggest Rose Bowl crowd ever, 103,839 people, rose up cheering as Stanford made an early thrust. An end-around run by Eric Cross gained 41 yards. Then Stanford's Jackie Brown galloped over the goal line. A good kick made it 7-0.

Later, Stanford scored again on a field goal by Steve Horowitz. But the Buckeyes had not become No. 1 in the nation by bowing meekly to underdogs. Woody's warriors bounced back. At half-time, they were ahead, 17-10.

In the third quarter, Stanford's prize toe, Steve Horowitz, kicked a record-breaking 48-yard field goal. It was 17-13, Ohio State. Grinding his teeth in rage, Woody Hayes urged his Buckeyes on. They

Michigan coach Bo Schlembechler admonishes his troops before the Rose Bowl game.

USC flanker Bob Chandler (10) scores against Michigan.

moved on the ground as the third period drew to a close. The Bucks made it to fourth down and inches to go on the Stanford 19. Big John Brockington tried to bulldoze his way through, but he was stopped by Stanford's Ron Kadziel.

When Stanford took possession, quarterback Jim Plunkett showed why he was the year's Heisman Trophy winner. Again and again he fired accurate passes and connected with his main receivers, Randy Vataha and Bob Moore.

On one play, Moore was closely guarded by two Buckeye defenders on the 4-yard line. Plunkett fired a pass, and Moore leaped into the air like a jack-in-the-box to spear the ball! A few moments later, Jackie Brown ran the ball into the end zone for a touchdown.

It was impossible, but it was happening! Stanford had gone ahead, 20-17!

And they didn't stop. Jack Schultz, a Stanford safety, made a big interception. It set up another Plunkett-to-Vataha connection that ended with little Randy scooting for a clinching touchdown. At the end, it was Stanford 27, Ohio State 17.

Before that Rose Bowl game, Coach Woody Hayes had reminded reporters that he had won in his three previous Rose Bowl appearances. "You can't beat my luck," he had chortled; but in 1971, in Pasadena, Woody's luck ran out.

What was worse, it was destined to stay out in Rose Bowl competition for quite a while. Michigan got the 1972 bid and got licked by Stanford. Ohio State came back in 1973 only to receive a fearful 42-17 drubbing from USC. Woody Hayes wanted revenge!

Woody Hayes was the coach to beat in the Rose Bowl.

Woody's Biggest Victory

Ohio State went to the Rose Bowl in 1974 under a cloud. Both the Buckeyes and Michigan had gone undefeated that season. In their last game against each other, they had tied at 10-10. The Big 10 brass had to decide which team would get the Pasadena bid.

Ohio State won the vote, but Michigan's howls echoed around the nation. Woody Hayes stopped his ears. All he wanted was a chance to lick USC. The rivalry between the two schools was as hot as that between the 5th century Romans and the Huns, and guess who was type-cast as Attila?

With the score tied, 21-21, the game was up for grabs when Ohio State made the ultimate push. Buckeye Neil Colzie returned a punt 56 yards. A few plays after that, with the ball on the Trojan 1-yard line, Ohio's Cornelius Greene faked brilliantly. Everyone thought he had given the ball to Pete Johnson. But Greene still had it; and while the Trojans pursued the Trojan Horse, Greene went over for a touchdown.

Ohio State speedster Archie Griffin ran 25 yards to the USC 2 not long afterward. Two plays later, Bruce Elia went over, and it was 35-21, Ohio State.

Coach Hayes goes for a ride after Ohio State won the 1974 Rose Bowl game.

In the fourth quarter, sophomore tailback Griffin did it again! This time, he performed a perfect broken-field run for 47 yards, wrapping up the game, 42-21.

"This was my topper," Woody Hayes said, "the greatest victory I've ever had."

A Trojan Triumph

The Trojans hoped for a big comeback the next season, but things started badly when they lost their very first game to the underdog Arkansas Razorbacks. One hometown headline read:

TROJANS' DREAM OF NO. 1 IS JUST HOGWASH, 22-7

But the USC squad didn't lose any more games, although they tied one. They finished top-rated in the nation and boasted one of the smartest college quarterbacks, Pat Haden, who was named a Rhodes Scholar. Haden's closest friend on the team was John McKay, Jr., son of the coach! The two boys were destined to play a historic part in the exciting 1975 Rose Bowl game.

Once again, it was USC vs. Ohio State. The Trojans got on the board in the first quarter with a field goal by Chris Limahelu, an Indonesian kicker. Ohio State bungled a field-goal attempt of their own. But then they took over on the USC 17, and not long afterward Ohio's Champ Henson went over for a touchdown. With just 31 seconds left in the half, it was Ohio State 7, USC 3.

Limahelu kicked a 39-yard field goal, while Ohio was off-side. Gambling for a big score, USC's Coach McKay decided to trade it for a first down on the Ohio 16. Then he watched in frustration as his boys met a stone wall of Buckeye defense. The Trojans had to try for another field goal, and this time they missed.

After a scoreless third quarter, Haden connected with Jim Obradovich at the climax of a 72-yard drive, putting USC ahead 10-7.

Joy reigns in California as USC's Shelton Diggs (26) converts for 2 points in the last moments of the 1975 Rose Bowl game. Moments earlier, John McKay (25) scored a touchdown. The Trojans upset the Bucks 18-17.

The Bucks' Van DeCree (88) tackles Anthony Davis of USC early in the 1975 Rose Bowl game when the California team seemed a hopeless underdog.

Shelton Diggs of USC holds the ball high after catching a last-minute 2-point conversion pass. It won the 1975 Rose Bowl game.

Ohio State quarterback Cornelius Greene answered with a thrust of his own, scampering 24 yards on a keeper play and marching his men another 53 yards to the Trojan 3. There the quarterback toted the ball across the goal line himself. With a good boot, it was 14-10, Buckeyes.

Shortly afterward, Ohio got into field-goal position and won another 3 points, making it 17-10. It looked as though they were headed for their second victory in a row.

Just 2 minutes remained. Trojan quarterback Haden sent a 38-yard pass to his pal, young John McKay, who caught the ball in the far right corner of the end zone.

The score was now 17-16, and Coach John McKay, Sr. had to decide whether to try for a single point with a kick, or a 2-pointer via a run or pass from the 2-yard line. In 1967, such a 2-point conversion attempt had failed; and the Trojans had lost a squeaker to Purdue. But there was no question but that they would try again in 1975. What good would a 17-17 tie be?

Haden had the ball moved to the left hashmark. He took the snap and rolled right. Haden began to scramble as both McKay and flanker Shelton Diggs broke for the end zone. Diggs came up clean, and Haden sent the ball in low. Diggs dived, caught it, and converted for 18-17, USC.

In the remaining time, Ohio State tried valiantly for a field goal, but it wasn't to be. Coach McKay summed it up, "It was a great game between two great teams. We were fortunate to win. They were unfortunate to lose."

Coming Up Roses

For the first half of the game, the 1976 Rose Bowl contest looked like a yawner.

Once again, Woody Hayes and his Buckeyes — undefeated that season — represented the Big 10. The Pac-8 team was UCLA's Bruins, led by young Coach Dick Vermeil. The Bruins had a good defense, but they weren't given a prayer against the mighty Bucks. Three months earlier, Woody's Ohio State lads had stomped UCLA, 41-20.

In the first two periods of the 1976 Rose Bowl, the Bruins contained Ohio to a single field goal. But the UCLA offense gained only 48 yards and Coast fans gloomily awaited the second-half slaughter.

But when UCLA returned, it was a new team! Less than 3 minutes into the third quarter, UCLA booted a field goal and it was 3-3. Then Bruin quarterback John Sciarra led a fast assault that got a touchdown in 6 plays. It was 9-3, Bruins.

They turned over the ball on a fumble. But on their next possession, they went all the way again. A long pass from Sciarra to flanker Wally Henry yielded a touchdown. With a good kick, it was 16-3.

The enraged Bruins countered with a TD of their own during the fourth period, but any recovery hopes were dashed when UCLA's Wendell Tyler galloped 54 yards to score again.

In the last minute, Woody Hayes called time out. He strode across the field and congratulated Coach Dick Vermeil. Then he vanished as everything came up roses for underdog UCLA, 23-10.

More than 100,000 Rose Bowl fans watch bandsmen spell out the letters "USA".

Kermit Alexander of UCLA rushes during the 1962 Rose Bowl classic. Minnesota won this game, 21-3.

Dancer Ann Miller rides on a flowery float during a Rose Parade.

Thousands of living flowers are used to make each Rose Parade float.

Rose Bowl Winners

1902 Michigan 49, Stanford 0
1916 Wash. State 14, Brown 0
1917 Oregon 14, Pennsylvania 0
1918 Marines 19, Camp Lewis 7
1919 Great Lakes 17, Marines 0
1920 Harvard 7, Oregon 6
1921 Calif. 28, Ohio State 0
1922 Calif. 0, Wash. & Jeff. 0
1923 USC 14, Penn State 3*
1924 Wash. 14, Navy 14
1925 Notre Dame 27, Stanford 10
1926 Ala. 20, Wash. 19
1927 Stanford 7, Ala. 7
1928 Stanford 7, Pittsburgh 6
1929 Ga. Tech. 8, Calif. 7
1930 USC 47, Pittsburgh 14
1931 Ala. 24, Wash. State 0
1932 USC 21, Tulane 12
1933 USC 35, Pittsburgh 0
1934 Columbia 7, Stanford 0
1935 Ala. 29, Stanford 13
1936 Stanford 7, SMU 0
1937 Pittsburgh 21, Wash. 0
1938 Calif. 13, Ala. 0
1939 USC 7, Duke 3
1940 USC 14, Tenn. 0
1941 Stanford 21, Nebr. 13
1942 Ore. State 20, Duke 16**
1943 Ga. 9, UCLA 0
1944 USC 29, Wash. 0
1945 USC 25, Tenn. 0
1946 Ala. 34, USC 14
1947 Illinois 45, UCLA 14
1948 Mich. 49, USC 0
1949 Northwestern 20, Calif. 14
1950 Ohio State 17, Calif. 14
1951 Mich. 14, USC 0
1952 Ill. 40, Stanford 7
1953 USC 7, Wisc. 0
1954 Mich. State 28, UCLA 20
1955 Ohio State 20, USC 7
1956 Mich. State 17, UCLA 14
1957 Iowa 35, Ore. State 19
1958 Ohio State 10, Ore. 7
1959 Iowa 38, Calif. 12
1960 Wash. 44, Wisc. 8
1961 Wash. 17, Minn. 7
1962 Minn. 21, UCLA 3
1963 USC 42, Wisc. 27
1964 Ill. 17, Wash. 7
1965 Mich. 34, Ore. State 7
1966 UCLA 14, Mich. State 12
1967 Purdue 14, USC 13
1968 USC 14, Ind. 3
1969 Ohio State 27, USC 16
1970 USC 10, Mich. 3
1971 Stanford 27, Ohio State 17
1972 Stanford 13, Mich. 12
1973 USC 42, Ohio State 17
1974 Ohio State 42, USC 21
1975 USC 18, Ohio State 17
1976 UCLA 23, Ohio State 10

*First game played in Rose Bowl Stadium.
**Game played in Duke Stadium, Durham, N.C. because of wartime restrictions.

SPORTS CLASSICS

WORLD SERIES
U.S. OPEN GOLF CHAMPIONSHIP
WIMBLEDON TENNIS TOURNAMENT
KENTUCKY DERBY
INDIANAPOLIS 500
OLYMPIC GAMES
SUPER BOWL
MASTERS TOURNAMENT OF GOLF
STANLEY CUP
NBA PLAY-OFFS
ROSE BOWL
AMERICA'S CUP YACHT RACE
WINTER OLYMPICS
PGA CHAMPIONSHIP TOURNAMENT
TRIPLE CROWN
AMERICAN TENNIS CHAMPIONSHIP
DAYTONA 500
GRAND PRIX
BOXING'S HEAVYWEIGHT CHAMPIONSHIP

CREATIVE EDUCATION